EMMANUEL JOSEPH

Baking Bliss: Sweet and Savory Creations for Every Craving

Copyright © 2025 by Emmanuel Joseph

All rights reserved. No part of this publication may be reproduced, stored or transmitted in any form or by any means, electronic, mechanical, photocopying, recording, scanning, or otherwise without written permission from the publisher. It is illegal to copy this book, post it to a website, or distribute it by any other means without permission.

First edition

This book was professionally typeset on Reedsy.
Find out more at reedsy.com

Contents

1	Chapter 1: The Foundations of Baking	1
2	Chapter 2: Essential Baking Tools and Equipment	2
3	Chapter 3: The Science of Baking	3
4	Chapter 4: Classic Sweet Treats	4
5	Chapter 5: Decadent Desserts	5
6	Chapter 6: Savory Bakes	6
7	Chapter 7: Healthy Baking	7
8	Chapter 8: Gluten-Free Baking	8
9	Chapter 9: Vegan Baking	10
10	Chapter 10: Baking for Special Occasions	11
11	Chapter 11: International Baking Delights	12
12	Chapter 12: The Joy of Baking Together	14

1

Chapter 1: The Foundations of Baking

Baking is an art that has been cherished for centuries, evolving through generations of passionate bakers. The foundation of baking lies in understanding the basic ingredients—flour, sugar, eggs, and butter—and how they interact to create delicious treats. This chapter explores these essential ingredients, their roles in baking, and how to choose the best quality for your recipes.

Flour is the backbone of most baked goods, providing structure and texture. Understanding the different types of flour, such as all-purpose, bread, and cake flour, is crucial for achieving the desired outcome in your baking. This chapter delves into the characteristics of each type and offers tips on how to use them effectively.

Sugar is not just a sweetener; it also affects the texture and moisture of your baked goods. This chapter explores the various types of sugar, including granulated, brown, and powdered sugar, and their unique properties. It also covers alternative sweeteners like honey and maple syrup, offering guidance on how to substitute them in your recipes.

Eggs and butter are the unsung heroes of baking, providing richness, moisture, and flavor. This chapter discusses the importance of these ingredients and how to use them to achieve the best results. It also includes tips on substituting eggs and butter for those with dietary restrictions, ensuring that everyone can enjoy the joys of baking.

2

Chapter 2: Essential Baking Tools and Equipment

Every successful baker needs a well-equipped kitchen. Having the right tools and equipment can make all the difference in the outcome of your baked goods. This chapter provides a comprehensive guide to the essential baking tools and equipment, from measuring cups and spoons to mixers and ovens.

Measuring accurately is key to successful baking. This chapter covers the importance of having a good set of measuring cups and spoons, as well as a reliable kitchen scale. It also offers tips on how to measure ingredients correctly, ensuring that your recipes turn out perfectly every time.

Mixing and blending ingredients is another critical step in baking. This chapter explores the different types of mixers, from handheld to stand mixers, and their various attachments. It also includes tips on how to mix ingredients properly, whether you're making a simple cake batter or a complex bread dough.

Ovens are the heart of any baking kitchen. This chapter discusses the different types of ovens, including conventional, convection, and steam ovens, and their pros and cons. It also provides tips on how to calibrate and maintain your oven, ensuring that your baked goods are cooked evenly and to perfection.

3

Chapter 3: The Science of Baking

Baking is as much a science as it is an art. Understanding the scientific principles behind baking can help you achieve consistent and delicious results. This chapter delves into the science of baking, exploring concepts like leavening agents, gluten formation, and the Maillard reaction.

Leavening agents, such as baking powder, baking soda, and yeast, are responsible for making your baked goods rise. This chapter explains how these agents work and how to use them effectively in your recipes. It also covers the differences between chemical and biological leavening agents, helping you choose the right one for your needs.

Gluten formation is a critical aspect of baking, particularly in bread and pastries. This chapter discusses the role of gluten in providing structure and elasticity to your baked goods. It also offers tips on how to develop gluten properly, whether you're kneading bread dough or folding pastry.

The Maillard reaction is a complex chemical process that occurs during baking, responsible for the browning and flavor development of your baked goods. This chapter explains how the Maillard reaction works and how to harness it to achieve the perfect golden crust on your breads and pastries.

4

Chapter 4: Classic Sweet Treats

Sweet treats are the heart and soul of baking, bringing joy and comfort to those who indulge in them. This chapter explores classic sweet treats, from cookies and cakes to pies and tarts, offering recipes and tips for creating these beloved desserts.

Cookies are a timeless favorite, loved by people of all ages. This chapter includes recipes for classic cookies like chocolate chip, oatmeal raisin, and sugar cookies, as well as tips for achieving the perfect texture and flavor. It also offers variations and twists on these classic recipes, allowing you to experiment and create your own signature cookies.

Cakes are the centerpiece of any celebration, from birthdays to weddings. This chapter provides recipes for classic cakes like vanilla, chocolate, and red velvet, along with tips for making moist and flavorful cakes. It also covers techniques for frosting and decorating your cakes, helping you create show-stopping desserts.

Pies and tarts are the epitome of comfort food, with their flaky crusts and delicious fillings. This chapter includes recipes for classic pies like apple, cherry, and pumpkin, as well as tips for making the perfect pie crust. It also offers variations on these classic recipes, such as savory tarts and galettes, providing inspiration for your baking adventures.

5

Chapter 5: Decadent Desserts

Decadent desserts are the ultimate indulgence, offering rich and luxurious flavors that satisfy even the most discerning sweet tooth. This chapter explores a range of decadent desserts, from chocolate truffles and mousse to crème brûlée and tiramisu, providing recipes and tips for creating these exquisite treats.

Chocolate is the star of many decadent desserts, with its rich and complex flavors. This chapter includes recipes for chocolate truffles, mousse, and lava cakes, as well as tips for working with chocolate to achieve the perfect texture and flavor. It also covers techniques for tempering chocolate, ensuring that your creations are smooth and glossy.

Custard-based desserts, such as crème brûlée and flan, offer a delicate and creamy contrast to richer desserts. This chapter provides recipes for these classic desserts, along with tips for achieving the perfect custard texture. It also includes variations on these recipes, such as adding flavored extracts or liqueurs for a unique twist.

Layered desserts, such as tiramisu and trifle, are a feast for both the eyes and the taste buds. This chapter includes recipes for these show-stopping desserts, along with tips for layering and assembling them. It also offers variations on these classic recipes, allowing you to experiment with different flavors and textures.

Chapter 6: Savory Bakes

Baking isn't just about sweet treats – savory bakes are just as delicious and satisfying. This chapter explores a range of savory bakes, from breads and pastries to casseroles and quiches, providing recipes and tips for creating these savory delights.

Breads are the cornerstone of any meal, offering a satisfying and versatile base for a variety of dishes. This chapter includes recipes for classic breads like baguettes, sourdough, and focaccia, as well as tips for achieving the perfect crust and crumb. It also covers techniques for kneading and shaping bread dough, helping you create artisanal-quality loaves at home.

Pastries, such as croissants and savory pies, offer a rich and flaky contrast to sweet treats. This chapter provides recipes for these classic pastries, along with tips for achieving the perfect pastry texture. It also includes variations on these recipes, such as adding savory fillings or incorporating whole grains for a healthier twist.

Casseroles and quiches are the epitome of comfort food, with their hearty and satisfying flavors. This chapter includes recipes for classic casseroles like lasagna and shepherd's pie, as well as tips for assembling and baking them. It also offers recipes for quiches and savory tarts, providing inspiration for your savory baking adventures.

7

Chapter 7: Healthy Baking

Baking doesn't have to be indulgent – it can also be healthy and nutritious. This chapter explores a range of healthy baking recipes, from whole grain breads and muffins to low-sugar cookies and cakes, providing tips and techniques for creating delicious and wholesome baked goods.

Whole grains are a great way to add nutrition and flavor to your baking. This chapter includes recipes for whole grain breads and muffins, as well as tips for incorporating whole grains into your favorite recipes. It also covers the benefits of whole grains, such as their high fiber content and rich flavor.

Reducing sugar is another way to make your baking healthier. This chapter provides tips for reducing sugar in your recipes, as well as recipes for low-sugar cookies and cakes. It also explores alternative sweeteners, such as stevia and monk fruit, and how to use them in your baking.

Incorporating fruits and vegetables into your baking is a great way to add nutrition and flavor. This chapter includes recipes for baked goods with fruits and vegetables, such as zucchini bread and carrot cake, as well as tips for using these ingredients effectively. It also covers the benefits of fruits and vegetables, such as their high nutrient content and natural sweetness.

8

Chapter 8: Gluten-Free Baking

Gluten-free baking can be challenging, but it doesn't have to be. This chapter provides a comprehensive guide to gluten-free baking, from selecting the right flours and ingredients to creating delicious and satisfying baked goods that everyone can enjoy.

The key to successful gluten-free baking is understanding the properties of different gluten-free flours and how they interact with other ingredients. This chapter provides an overview of the most common gluten-free flours, such as almond flour, rice flour, and coconut flour, along with tips for using them effectively in your recipes.

Binders and thickeners, such as xanthan gum and guar gum, play a crucial role in gluten-free baking, providing structure and elasticity to your baked goods. This chapter explains how to use these ingredients and offers tips for achieving the perfect texture and consistency in your gluten-free recipes.

In addition to individual ingredients, this chapter also covers the use of gluten-free baking mixes and pre-made blends. It includes recipes for classic gluten-free baked goods like bread, cookies, and cakes, along with tips for customizing them to suit your taste preferences. Whether you're new to gluten-free baking or a seasoned pro, this chapter will provide you with the knowledge and inspiration you need.

In addition to individual ingredients, this chapter also covers the use of gluten-free baking mixes and pre-made blends. It includes recipes for classic

CHAPTER 8: GLUTEN-FREE BAKING

gluten-free baked goods like bread, cookies, and cakes, along with tips for customizing them to suit your taste preferences. Whether you're new to gluten-free baking or a seasoned pro, this chapter will provide you with the knowledge and inspiration you need.

Experimenting with gluten-free baking can be a rewarding experience, allowing you to discover new flavors and textures. This chapter offers tips for adapting your favorite recipes to be gluten-free, as well as advice on how to troubleshoot common issues. It also includes suggestions for gluten-free substitutions and alternatives, helping you to create delicious and satisfying baked goods without gluten.

Finally, this chapter provides guidance on how to maintain a gluten-free kitchen, ensuring that your baked goods are safe for those with gluten sensitivities. It covers everything from selecting gluten-free ingredients to preventing cross-contamination, helping you create a gluten-free environment that is both safe and enjoyable.

9

Chapter 9: Vegan Baking

Vegan baking is a delicious and compassionate way to enjoy your favorite baked goods without using animal products. This chapter explores the essentials of vegan baking, from selecting the right ingredients to creating delicious and satisfying treats that everyone can enjoy.

The key to successful vegan baking is understanding how to replace traditional ingredients like eggs, butter, and milk with plant-based alternatives. This chapter provides an overview of the most common vegan substitutes, such as flax eggs, coconut oil, and almond milk, along with tips for using them effectively in your recipes.

In addition to individual ingredients, this chapter also covers the use of pre-made vegan baking mixes and plant-based products. It includes recipes for classic vegan baked goods like cookies, cakes, and muffins, along with tips for customizing them to suit your taste preferences. Whether you're new to vegan baking or a seasoned pro, this chapter will provide you with the knowledge and inspiration you need.

Experimenting with vegan baking can be a fun and rewarding experience, allowing you to discover new flavors and textures. This chapter offers tips for adapting your favorite recipes to be vegan, as well as advice on how to troubleshoot common issues. It also includes suggestions for vegan substitutions and alternatives, helping you create delicious and satisfying baked goods without animal products.

10

Chapter 10: Baking for Special Occasions

Baking for special occasions is a wonderful way to show your love and appreciation for those you care about. This chapter explores the art of baking for celebrations, from birthdays and weddings to holidays and family gatherings. It provides recipes and tips for creating show-stopping desserts that will make any occasion memorable.

Birthdays are a time for celebration, and nothing says "happy birthday" like a homemade cake. This chapter includes recipes for classic birthday cakes, as well as tips for decorating and personalizing them. It also offers ideas for themed cakes and cupcakes, allowing you to create a unique and festive dessert for any birthday celebration.

Weddings are a special occasion that calls for an equally special dessert. This chapter provides recipes for elegant wedding cakes and desserts, along with tips for achieving a professional finish. It also includes ideas for customizing your wedding cake to suit your theme and style, ensuring that your dessert is a perfect reflection of your big day.

Holidays and family gatherings are the perfect time to indulge in your favorite baked goods. This chapter includes recipes for holiday classics like gingerbread cookies, pumpkin pie, and fruitcake, as well as tips for making these treats extra special. It also offers ideas for creating festive and delicious desserts for any holiday celebration.

11

Chapter 11: International Baking Delights

Baking is a universal language that transcends cultural boundaries, with each country offering its unique and delicious baked goods. This chapter explores a variety of international baking delights, from French pastries and Italian biscotti to Middle Eastern baklava and Japanese mochi. It provides recipes and tips for creating these global treats in your own kitchen.

French baking is renowned for its elegance and sophistication, with pastries like croissants, éclairs, and macarons capturing the hearts of dessert lovers worldwide. This chapter includes recipes for these classic French pastries, as well as tips for achieving the perfect texture and flavor. It also covers techniques for mastering French baking, such as laminating dough and making choux pastry.

Italian baking is characterized by its rustic simplicity and rich flavors. This chapter provides recipes for classic Italian baked goods like biscotti, cannoli, and panettone, along with tips for making them at home. It also explores the role of regional ingredients and traditions in Italian baking, offering inspiration for your culinary adventures.

Middle Eastern baking offers a delightful array of flavors and textures, with desserts like baklava, ma'amoul, and kanafeh. This chapter includes recipes for these traditional Middle Eastern treats, along with tips for working with ingredients like phyllo dough and rose water. It also provides guidance on

CHAPTER 11: INTERNATIONAL BAKING DELIGHTS

creating authentic flavors and presentations, bringing the essence of Middle Eastern baking to your kitchen.

12

Chapter 12: The Joy of Baking Together

Baking is a joyful and communal activity that brings people together, creating lasting memories and delicious treats. This final chapter celebrates the joy of baking with others, from family baking sessions and bake sales to baking clubs and virtual baking parties. It offers ideas and tips for making baking a fun and collaborative experience.

Family baking sessions are a wonderful way to bond and create memories with your loved ones. This chapter includes ideas for family-friendly baking projects, such as cookie decorating, cupcake making, and bread baking. It also offers tips for involving children in the baking process, making it a fun and educational activity for all ages.

Bake sales are a great way to share your love of baking with your community while raising funds for a good cause. This chapter provides tips for organizing a successful bake sale, from choosing the right recipes to packaging and presenting your baked goods. It also includes ideas for themed bake sales and creative ways to attract customers.

Baking clubs and virtual baking parties are a fun and social way to connect with fellow baking enthusiasts. This chapter offers ideas for starting your own baking club, whether in-person or online, and tips for organizing baking events and challenges. It also includes suggestions for virtual baking parties, allowing you to bake and share your creations with friends and family, no matter where they are.

www.ingramcontent.com/pod-product-compliance
Lightning Source LLC
LaVergne TN
LVHW010446070526
838199LV00066B/6225